My
SPECIAL

Book for Mum!

Written by

....

© The Life Graduate Publishing Group

All Rights Reserved

No part of this book may be scanned, reproduced or distributed in any printed or electronic form without the prior permission of the author or publisher.

About the Author

That's me!

My Name is _____

I am _____ **Yrs old:**

My Favorite thing to do is:

_____
_____
_____
_____
_____

Mum, I wrote this book for you because

_____
_____
_____
_____
_____

#01

MUM, I LOVE YOU BECAUSE....

#02

MUM, YOU ARE FUNNY WHEN....

#03

THIS IS MY FAVOURITE PHOTO OF US

Stick photo here!

#04

MY FAVOURITE PLACE TO VISIT WITH YOU IS....

#05
THIS IS A DRAWING OF US TOGETHER!

#06

THIS IS A TRACING OF MY HAND!

trace your hand here

#07
MUM, THESE ARE 3 THINGS THAT YOU DO THAT ARE KIND

#1 _____

#2 _____

#3 _____

there are lots more too!!

#08

WE CELEBRATE YOUR BIRTHDAY ON..

MONTH............................

DAY................................

#09

YOU COOK THE BEST..

#10

MY FAVORITE STORY IS....

I love stories!

#11

I SOMETIMES GET A LITTLE BIT SCARED WHEN....

but i'm still very brave!

#12

MUM, I WOULD LIKE YOU TO SHOW ME HOW TO........

#13

I THINK YOUR FAVORITE TIME OF THE YEAR IS...

BECAUSE....

#14

MUM, I THINK YOU ARE THE BEST AT...

#15
THIS DRAWING IS OF US TOGETHER AT

_____

#16

YOUR FAVORITE FOOD IS........

#17

IF I COULD GET YOU ANYTHING IN THE WHOLE WIDE WORLD, IT WOULD BE.......

#18

THIS BOOK WAS MADE ESPECIALLY FOR YOU ON

Day..............................

Month..........................

Year.............................

I am .... years old

SPECIAL
MOMENTS

iNSERT PHOTOS

SPECIAL
MOMENTS

insert photos

Notes

Notes

books in the

JR. AUTHOR SERIES
 Perfect for our little authors!

 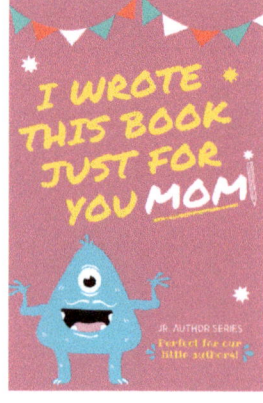 

www.ingramcontent.com/pod-product-compliance
Lightning Source LLC
LaVergne TN
LVHW051935070526
838200LV00077B/4643